"The first time I glanced in the mirror and saw my father looking back at me was terrifying. *A Funny Thing Happened on My Way to Old Age* is humorous but gives serious help. I will view the image in the mirror with less terror, more tolerance and hope."

JERRY COOK, AUTHOR OF *LOVE, ACCEPTANCE AND FORGIVENESS*

"Stan's keen wit and lucid entertaining style make his insights as enjoyable as they are thought provoking."

GARY BRUMBELOW, DIRECTOR, INTERACT MINISTRIES

"Stanley Baldwin proves once and for all that moving past 50 need not threaten your body, soul or funny bone. Grab your bifocals and hang on."

PHIL CALLAWAY, AUTHOR AND EDITOR OF *SERVANT* MAGAZINE

"If you have not faced up to passing 50 yet, you will. Stan Baldwin provides entertaining and thoughtful approaches to dealing with the changes and trials you will face."

VERNAL WILKINSON, VILLAGE MISSIONS DISTRICT REPRESENTATIVE

"In this book Stanley Baldwin tackles common misconceptions about life after 50. The witty personal stories of his spiritual journey will inspire those of any age."

DR. DORIS BROUGHAM, PRESIDENT AND FOUNDER, OVERSEAS RADIO AND TELEVISION

"Stan opened my eyes to a deeper understanding by allowing me a glimpse at aging from my parents' vantage point. Wonderfully written—I recommend it to all whose parents are getting on in life."

DR. MARK HOEFFNER, GENERAL DIRECTOR, CB NORTHWEST

D0973279

"Unless you die young, your aging is inevitable. Stan shows how you can not only endure but shine. I recommend this book to everyone, no matter how young or old."

JEANNE HALSEY, WRITER

"Stan Baldwin was my boss and pastor when I was a pup, and he taught me many lessons about work and writing and life. Still at the top of his game in *A Funny Thing Happened on My Way to Old Age,* he's mentoring me to finish well. You'll laugh, you'll identify, you'll 'aha,' and you'll read it from cover to cover."

JERRY B. JENKINS, COAUTHOR OF THE LEFT BEHIND SERIES

"Most of us don't think about being over the hill until we're rolling briskly down the other side. Stan's book combines wit, wisdom and a wacky look at the later years."

MARION STROUD, AUTHOR, BEDFORD, ENGLAND

Stanley C. Baldwin

A Funny Thing Happened on My Way to Old Age

LIFE CHANGES AFTER 50

InterVarsity Press
Downers Grove, Illinois

InterVarsity Press
P.O. Box 1400, Downers Grove, IL 60515-1426
World Wide Web: www.ivpress.com
E-mail: mail@ivpress.com

InterVarsity Press® is the book-publishing division of InterVarsity Christian Fellowship/USA®,
a student movement active on campus at hundreds of universities, colleges and schools of nursing in the
United States of America, and a member movement of the International Fellowship of Evangelical
Students. For information about local and regional activities, write Public Relations Dept., InterVarsity
Christian Fellowship/USA, 6400 Schroeder Rd., P.O. Box 7895, Madison, WI 53707-7895, or visit
the IVCF website at <www.intervarsity.org>.

Design: Cindy Kiple

Images: Digital Vision/Getty Images
         Photodisc/Getty Images
         Rubberball Productions/Getty Images

ISBN 0-8308-3278-5

Printed in the United States of America ∞

Library of Congress Cataloging-in-Publication Data

Baldwin, Stanley C.
 A funny thing happened on my way to old age: life changes after 50
 / By Stanley C. Baldwin.
    p. cm.
 ISBN 0-8308-3278-5 (pbk.: alk. paper)
 1. Older Christians—Religious life. 2. Aging—Religious
 aspects—Christianity. I. Title.
 BV4580.B25 2005
 248.8'5—dc22

                                                              2004025506

P	16	15	14	13	12	11	10	9	8	7	6	5	4	3	2	1
Y	16	15	14	13	12	11	10	09	08	07	06	05				

To all of you who have felt

the hot breath of aging on your back,

whether at thirty or fifty or seventy.

Stanley C. Baldwin

Contents

I Hate Growing Old— But I Love Those Perks

I t started almost fifteen years ago. My wife, Marj, and I had moved to a new community and visited a local church. We arrived for Sunday school, were warmly greeted and then ushered into a class of *seniors*. To say I was displeased is an understatement akin to calling an ax-murderer "an undesirable." At the following worship service, I wrote on my visitor's card that we would not be back if we had to attend that class. Message received. The next Sunday we were directed into a class of middle-aged adults, where obviously we belonged.

Unfortunately, the assault on our prime-of-life status from every quarter of society has only intensified since then. Waitresses have stopped asking if we qualify for the senior discount; they simply give it to us. When I'm in public young women step aside for *me to enter doors ahead of them.* And then there are the "opportunities" offered us. Wouldn't we like to go with this or that tour group *on a bus?* Just think, we could leave that miserable driving to someone else along with all the planning and arrangements. Evidently we would still have to dress ourselves.

To me the whole idea had all the appeal of a visit to the dentist. Not that there's anything wrong with bus excursions, *if we were elderly.*

Even people who know me well began to be caught up in the delusion. One was Sandy Cathcart, a warm friend since 1989 and my successor as director of the Oregon Christian Writers summer conference. Sandy was present when I gave the major address at an OCW winter conference not long ago. She came to me afterward to say how good it was. "And you still speak with a lot of energy," she said. I'm sure she meant it as a compliment.

A publisher issued a newly designed version of one of my books that had been in print for twenty years. On the back cover I was described as one who "remains active in writing and speaking." I wondered why they didn't add that I could still feed myself.

What was the matter with these people? Didn't they know that—pick your cliché—"you are only as old as you feel," "old age is a state of mind," "I'm not getting older, I'm getting better"?

FAULT LINES IN MY YOUTHFUL PERSONA

Call it the power of suggestion if you will, but eventually my body began to echo the opinions of society. Old age began to insist it was far more a stubborn fact than a state of mind. There was a time when I would jog circles around Marj as we went on our two-mile circuits together. I wanted to jog; she wanted to walk. Jogging circles around her was the only way we could do it together. That's now a dimming memory. Sometimes I struggle to keep pace with her.

The camera has also become less and less friendly. Who is that graying old guy? I mean we all take bad pictures sometimes, but this is getting ridiculous. Meanwhile, suspenders are becoming my valued companions. They hold up my pants without that annoying tightness around my waist.

And what about that face? Might I soon look like the late Ronald Reagan, my naturally handsome profile marred by sagging jowls? Probably not, but you know, I really might look good in a beard. It would also help disguise any wrinkles that sneakily appeared while I wasn't looking.

Of course, the beard turned out to be nearly white, but there's a solution for that. In just five minutes I can have a natural looking dark-brown beard. Better yet, the product doesn't just color my beard; it rejuvenates it. Says so right on the box.

Other fault lines began to appear in my youthful persona as well. Even my doctor contributed to the idea that I should be on the decline. At a routine but thorough physical exam, he asked how often my wife and I had sexual relations. When I told him, he was impressed. "That's good for a man your age." I didn't know whether to be pleased with the "that's good" or offended by the "man your age."

Unfortunately, since then I've become neither that good nor a man that age.

IT'S JUST NOT RIGHT

Part of my problem with this aging business is theological. Aging is a part of the death process, and I don't like it one bit. I don't think God made people to die. This stuff about "the natural cycle of life and death" doesn't appeal to me at all. Death is *not* natural. It's an enemy out to strip me of God's gift of life. I see the exuberance, the sense of wonder, the sheer delight of a small child and I know that's what *life* is supposed to be. And I want that. Oh, how I want that! So don't tell me to embrace aging.

Still, it chips away at me relentlessly. Psalm 90 is a great psalm that looks at life from a perspective near its end. Moses writes:

You sweep men away in the sleep of death;
    they are like the new grass of the morning—
though in the morning it springs up new,
    by evening it is dry and withered. (vv. 5-6)

Lindy Batdorf, in her book *Stop and Smell the Asphalt,* credits her grandmother with instilling in her a good attitude toward aging. "She helped me learn that we get to add new experiences to our lives, but somewhere inside we are always every age we have ever been."

I like that. I like it a lot. And it's true. I am still the boy who went barefoot and shirtless all summer in the sawmill town of Bend, Oregon, where I grew up. I am the boy who tasted my first candy bar when I ran over a Mounds on my bike and retrieved it only half smashed. I never dreamed anything could taste that good.

I am the youth who worked hard delivering the *Oregonian* newspaper every morning of the week even though it meant I had to get up at 4:30 a.m. to do it. And I am still the person who experienced turmoil in my teens and, later, great purpose in my career.

Still, the idea that aging equals enrichment is a bit sanguine. Moses' words ring every bit as true as those of Lindy's grandmother. He said that like grass we spring up in the morning and wither at evening. I like the idea of being every age I have ever been, but I really don't care for that withering part.

DENIAL WORKS ONLY SO LONG

A turning point for me came at a men's retreat where I was to speak five times between Friday evening and Sunday noon—a heavy schedule that I had no doubt I could handle. The Tigard Christian Church held the gathering annually at the Molalla Retreat Center, and I was their 2003 guest speaker.

What a great bunch of men! I had gone to inspire them, and I hope I did, but they certainly inspired me. For the most part these weren't demonstrative guys. What they were, though, was honest, open and deeply devoted to the Lord Jesus Christ. And young. I was probably about twenty years senior to the oldest of them.

Normally, when speaking at any function, I had ignored the elephant in the room—my obvious age. This time I came half to terms with it and began the first session by making fun of myself. I appropriated a joke I'd read on the Internet and applied it to me personally.

"I was talking with an old friend recently," I said, "and told him about my new hearing aid. 'State of the art and very expensive, but it has really helped. I hear almost normally again.'

"'What kind is it?' he asked.

"I looked at my wristwatch and said, '12:30.'"

They liked that one, so I launched right into another.

"You know, losing your hearing is bad

enough but losing your memory is even worse. My friend is getting forgetful. The other day we were visiting, and he said hesitantly, 'We've known each other for thirty years. I consider you one of the best friends I have in this world. I'm embarrassed and ashamed to tell you this but—I can't think of your name. Tell me, what is it?'

"I said, 'Hmmm, can you give me a minute?'"

They slapped their knees and roared with laughter. My acknowledging the elephant hadn't been so bad after all, when I made light of it. The next evening after my message the men gathered in small groups to share personal concerns and to pray for one another. For the first time I openly faced what I had been running from for a long time. When it came my turn to ask for prayer, I said, "I am grieving"—I paused—"over my lost youth."

It was something I hadn't realized until that moment, but then it was so clear, so unmistakable, I marveled that I had been so slow to see it. I was *grieving!*

Something about that insight was liberating to me. I still didn't like the idea of getting old, but I did recognize it as a fact I had to face. The denial was over. A new recognition had begun.

AGE HAS ITS PERKS

I still have not come entirely to the rosy view of old age Lindy Batdorf articulated. Or that the poet Robert Browning suggested when he wrote "Rabbi ben Ezra" in 1862:

> Grow old along with me!
> The best is yet to be,
> The last of life for which the first was made.

And what about that title Alex Comfort used for his 1990 book *Say Yes to Old Age?* How Pollyanna is that?

But there are good things about aging too. There's no use being so fixated on the negatives that I can't enjoy the advantages.

Did you know that seniors get a bigger personal exemption on their income taxes? And discounts at shows, restaurants, airlines and pharmacies? For a lifelong penny pincher like me, that's kind of nice. I must admit, though, that I'm not so sure I deserve it. A sign I saw at a marina made the point. "No, we don't give discounts to seniors; you have already had more time to make money than the rest of us."

I also see advantages far surpassing senior discounts, not the least of which is an increase of wisdom. I have simply lived long enough now to be immune to most scams (and many forms of the common cold). I also perceive that some banks, insurance companies, credit card companies and service companies of all kinds have more similarities to scam artists than differences from them. They still are mainly trying to get into my wallet as deep as they can and don't mind using deception to do it.

This insight is called "Read the fine print, look for the catch, and never buy into anything you haven't checked out."

I also notice an increased ability to work smarter instead of harder. I don't have the stamina I once had, but then I have found better and easier ways to do many tasks.

Since I can't work such long hours, I have more leisure time. That's a good thing. It is one of those good things of which more and more is not better and better, however. Too much leisure time ages you. In fact it's deadly.

Another valuable thing I have now that I never had before is a palpable happiness. I don't mean my life before age fifty was an unhappy one. Yet I don't recall ever getting up in the morning and spontaneously saying to myself, "You are a happy man," as I do from time to time now.

Maybe it's simply a case of appreciating my blessings more than I used to. Maybe it's like the old joke about being thankful for a toothache because it feels so good when it goes away. I get up feeling refreshed, not hurting badly anywhere, with a new day of opportunities ahead of me, and I am happy. Something about a fresh, new morning exhilarates me. Going out to get the morning newspaper, I smile, pump my fists in the air as a triumphant salute to God, and celebrate.

I can't really explain why I am happier now when I have serious health issues than in younger years when I didn't. I think, though, how Captain Allen Gardiner gave similar testimony under much worse circumstances than I ever face. Along with his entire six-man team, Gardiner died of cold and hunger trying to reach Patagonia with the gospel in 1851. In his journal were found these words, "Poor and weak as we are, our (beached) boat is very Bethel to our souls, for we feel and know that God is here. Asleep or awake, I am beyond the power of expression, happy."

LIFE IN ITS SECOND SEASON

Now that I've come to terms with the stubborn fact that I am aging, I think it's a bit like playing a second season in the game of life. I've survived the regular season and now I'm into the finals. It's still the same game, but the rules are a little different, and so am I.

This second season is important, because that's when championships are won or lost.

To address some of the differences we face in the second season will be my focus through the rest of this book. For example, we'll look at why grumpiness too often typifies older people and what we can do about it. I speak from experience. Despite my palpable happiness, I have my bouts with grumpiness too. Life is never simple!

A keener sense of our mortality is another mark of aging—one that almost everyone encounters. It can strike fear in our hearts and destroy what could otherwise still be very good days. Often the fear is realistic: death does stalk us. But as one friend told me not long ago, "Yes, I have a life-threatening illness, but I have decided to die only once." She unknowingly echoed Shakespeare, who wrote in *Julius Caesar,* "Cowards die many times before their deaths, the valiant never taste of death but once."

That same friend had an even greater struggle, however, with another age-related issue when the approaching end of her lifelong work threatened her identity. She and I and countless other seniors have wondered what use we have if we can no longer pursue our calling in life or do anything else of value for that matter. In one chapter you'll meet this particular friend and some others like her, and I'll share my own journey through "retirement depression" to a new sense of fulfillment.

We'll also look at changing times and circumstances that call for changes in us, unless we are simply to lose out early in life's second season. All of our lives we needed to be flexible and adapt to change, and that part is no different now. The difference is that when we get older we have a greater tendency to settle into a comfortable status quo. But we don't have to yield to that tendency. Embracing change can be liberating.

One of the stickiest elements of aging comes when our declining condition makes us dependent on others. That assaults our sense of worth and makes many elderly people fearful about going on. In my state, Oregon, we have the dubious distinction of being the first in the nation to legalize physician-assisted suicide. Studies show that most people who choose that option do so primarily because they worry that they will become totally dependent. They don't want to be such a burden on others. Becoming dependent is a big issue, then, but there are answers.

Bittersweet memories of loved ones who have died, leaving an empty spot deep in our hearts, is a nearly inevitable prospect for those who live to an advanced age. That circumstance has sometimes made me feel like an orphan. However, we can celebrate our memories of those loved ones even as we grieve our loss. Even better, we can anticipate a glad reunion in heaven.

The need to finish well our second season (and all of life) is the focus of my final chapter. Our declining years may well confront us with difficulties we have never faced before. Some of those are detailed in this book. They involve circumstances that are threatening, or at least sufficiently unpleasant, that none of us would welcome. For us there is this encouraging word from Psalm 27:

> The LORD is my light and my salvation—
> whom shall I fear?
> The LORD is the stronghold of my life—
> of whom shall I be afraid? . . .

Though war break out against me,
    even then will I be confident. . . .

For in the day of trouble
    he will keep me. . . .

 I am still confident of this:
     I will see the goodness of the Lord
     in the land of the living.
Wait for the LORD;
    be strong and take heart
    and wait for the LORD. (vv. 1, 3, 5, 13-14)

Twice the passage speaks of living with confidence. I can't think of a better companion than confidence to take with us as we trot out to the floor or field each day to play out our final season.

I Am Not a Grouch

From time to time during my aging years, my wife, Marj, has actually accused me of being a grouch. Of course, I am not and never was. The very idea that I could be one of those cranky, sour old people who does nothing but complain is enough to make me—well, grumpy.

A little reflection suggests that when we complain, 90 percent of the people don't care and don't want to hear it; the other 10 percent probably feel a secret satisfaction that we are getting what we deserve.

Old age is not a license to grumble. Of course, it wouldn't hurt if youngsters, those under fifty, realized there are sometimes understandable reasons for it. Old age has its attendant stresses, and people of any age tend to get cranky under stress. Even a child of sunny disposition may be a bear when a nap is needed. Or a diaper change. Or a feeding. It should come as no surprise then that coping with chronic pain or worry or sleeplessness is a bit hard on an older person's cheery demeanor.

Personally, though, I like to think I can fold my arms and declare with complete confidence that, to paraphrase former president Richard Nixon, "I am not a grouch."

OK, I suppose my irritation over little frustrations has increased a bit with the passing years. Grumpiness is something that can creep up on anybody. I've thought we should all be secretly taped—let us hear the edge in our voice, demonstrate that, yes, most of us do at times sound grouchy. (Though, of course, we aren't.)

My daughter Krystal has the solution for dealing with a grouch. When anyone demonstrates irritability around her, she smiles and says, "Rowrrr!" with a show of her fingers spread like cat claws. It lets them know how they are coming across.

I would do that, but by the time I think of it the moment has passed. You have to do that while the grouch's voice tones still hang in the air so he or she can't easily deny it.

A CASE FOR THE DEFENSE

As for me becoming more impatient and irritable with age, I plead innocent on grounds of extreme provocation. You would be impatient too if you were a victim of a cosmic conspiracy. It doesn't matter how carefully I choose the best line at the checkout counter, something will happen to delay me. A customer in front of me will have a dispute with the cashier. Or there will be some sudden malfunction of the register. The cashier will have to call for assistance; the whole line must wait while a manager-type vested with authority—and a key to unlock the register—comes and solves the problem.

Sometimes the customer just ahead of me has a sudden change of heart about the merchandise, and I am left to survey the less-than-edifying tabloids displayed beside the checkout line while someone from a distant department of the store brings the desired item to the register. At times, when nothing else goes wrong, a casual cashier will chat with a casual customer while I burn.

Please don't suggest I simply move to a

different checkout line. I am not stupid. I have certainly tried that. When I head for a line that looks shorter or faster, two things happen very quickly. My new line grinds to a halt, and the old one starts moving. As I told you, this situation has all the marks of a conspiracy.

This problem is so bad and so predictable that I have on occasion warned the customer behind me, "You might want to think about choosing a different line because this one is undoubtedly going to take a while."

When Marj is with me, we sometimes try to divide and conquer. She stands in one promising line while I stand in another. As a rule, she gets to the front of her line first (surprise, surprise), at which point she waves and summons me. Since I am a sensitive guy, this maneuver doesn't work well for me; I don't like the fierce looks I get from other customers when I maneuver my cart full of purchases in front of them.

It isn't just the stores that offend. Gas stations are also in on the plot. I can be quite sure that drivers who pull up to the pumps at the same time I do—and even some who pull up later—will leave ahead of me. I live in one of only two states that don't have self-service gas, so it isn't my fault I face all this unfairness and delay. Sometimes I avoid asking for a fill-up because if I say "fill 'er up," the attendant will set my pump on super slow and do *something* elsewhere while gasoline trickles into my tank. Eventually, the pump stops automatically because the tank is full, or there's another Mid-East war, whichever comes first. Then I still have to wait for the attendant to return and release me from the hose that tethers my car to his gas pump.

"The Lord must be trying to teach me patience," I have said more than once. That self-talk never did much good. I just felt all the more frustrated because I obviously wasn't learning my lesson.

GET OUTTA MY WAY!

During most of my life I have had some rationale for being "driven." I am a man on a mission. I have things to do—important things. One of them is *not* wasting time waiting in lines. Or stalled in traffic. Or having aimless people get in my way by blocking the store aisles or auto traffic lanes. Oh, I am courteous. I am glad to let people go ahead of me. That's fine, if they would just *go*. What I find maddening is their lollygagging in my way. How thoughtless!

I'm older now and more mellow, I think, but I'm still on a mission. I still have no time to waste. (At least not in ways that try my patience. To spend hours watching college football or playing computer games is not, as I have explained to Marj, a waste.)

I once had a glimpse of the sad effect impatience can have on others. Max was a missionary to Mexico when I met him, but he had been a gas station attendant in his pre-Christian days. One of his regular customers was an older professor from a nearby theological seminary. "What a grouch!" Max told me. "If it had been up to him, I never would have become a Christian."

Recalling that comment always gives me pause. Do I come across to service people the way the old seminary professor did to Max? But then I think, *Hey, the clerks who wait on me don't even know I am a Christian, so how could I be a stumbling block?*

Now there is a solution—don't let anyone know you are a Christian!

THE AHA! MOMENT

Lately I have factored something new into my thinking—something that helps change the way I behave when frustrated. This new insight has been far more helpful than telling myself I need to be patient or that I need to be a good Christian witness.

Look, I said to myself one day when I was feeling grumpy about a slow gas purchase. *Look, God has given you everything. You have your health. You have a loving wife and caring children. On Father's Day you will hear from every one of your five grown children. You have no worries about where your next meal is coming from. God has given you all of this and you are down in the mouth because you had to wait ten minutes at the gas pump.*

A thought came to me with great conviction. *I have been had! I have allowed a few trivial circumstances to steal my joy! How foolish!*

Previously, my thoughts about needing to change were prompted by guilt. Why couldn't I learn patience? Why wasn't I a better witness? This time was different. Not guilt but dismay came upon me. I purposed in my heart I would no longer forfeit my joy so easily.

With that breakthrough behind me, another soon followed. I realized it's not only unsatisfactory behavior of people that bugs me. Life is full of frustrations that have nothing to do with other people but are strictly issues between me and reality.

I can't string an extension cord or a garden hose for any appreciable distance around my yard without it hanging up on something, requiring me to retrace my steps to free it. Oh, I can whip it in the air and pull it harder with the hope that my determination will win the day. But usually, whipping the air won't work, and if I pull too hard, I'll have a repair or a new purchase on my hands.

There are all sorts of similar annoyances. For some reason—are my fingerprints wearing off?—I can hardly separate pages anymore. And opening those flimsy plastic bags in the produce department, forget it.

Gravity plays tricks on me too. I toss something, anything, on a surface not completely flat and it ends up on the floor. I drop a piece of wastepaper directly over the wastebasket, and something—a mysterious air current?—floats it onto the floor instead of into the basket.

While people can be difficult or can serve me poorly, this isn't a people problem. It's me versus the world the way God made it. If I won't let people steal my joy, how much more should I not let inanimate objects get the best of me?

The good news is, I now have a response that defuses these frustrations when they strike. This response strikes a truce with reality to replace my previous blind hostility toward it. "Law of physics," I say calmly when things don't go my way. By "law of physics," I mean the physical universe is working just the way God, for good reason, designed it. Then I proceed to do what the law of physics requires without useless complaining about it.

WHAT A DIFFERENCE IT MAKES!

Being a grouch is not just useless, it is destructive.

When I was a boy we lived next door to a grouchy old woman. She didn't like children, evidently, because when we played in the street in front of her house, she would crab at us and try to spray us with the garden hose. All that did was make us rise to the challenge and taunt her. Then one day her cesspool malfunctioned and began to seep raw sewage into the street. We were unmerciful in pointing out that she was violating the law, and we were going to report her.

In retrospect I realize that we were as much at fault as she was. We were behaving like brats, neither respectful nor compassionate toward this poor, unhappy old woman. Her grouchiness was destructive and stimulated a cruel response from us mean little kids.

Another old woman came into my life about that time. Grandma Morris was the antithesis of our crabby neighbor. She wasn't really my grandmother; I never knew any of my real grandparents. Grandma Morris was the mother of my new stepfather, and she lived on my paper route. On snowy, cold winter mornings she would meet me at her front porch and insist that I come in to warm my freezing hands. She would also have a cup of hot chocolate ready to warm me from the inside out.

I began to visit Grandma Morris often, not just while delivering papers. She always had time for me—and something good to eat. She could hardly get around anymore and would often ask me to get her a drink of cold water from the kitchen tap. Our town, Bend, Oregon, had the most delicious, pure, cold mountain water, and Grandma Morris always had the same instructions for me. "Let it run until it gets cold," she would say, long after I was thoroughly aware of her wishes.

In all the many hours I spent in the company of Grandma Morris, I never knew her to be unpleasant. The closest I ever heard to a complaint was an occasional lament about the way society was degenerating. Men and women were actually bathing together now (she called swimming bathing), and she thought that was scandalous.

When I was twelve, we moved away to Portland, and I never saw Grandma Morris again, but she had certainly filled a void in my life. Now I am a grandparent myself, with both grown-up grandchildren and little ones. My little grandkids may not know how blessed they are to have grandparents in their lives. They probably don't. But I know, so I'm there for them when, for example, they want me to hear all about their latest adventures or to play games. Marj, for her part, is the quintessential grandma, soft of heart and of lap, and how they love her.

Someday not long from now, these last grandchildren will be grown. They won't need me anymore and will be busy with lives of their own. But I hope they will remember me fondly once in a while. And if they do come to see me, I hope it won't be simply an unpleasant duty for them, but a pleasure.

Please, God, I don't want to be a sour, complaining old man. Make me the kind of person my children and grandchildren can enjoy. And one my wife won't accuse of being a grouch.

Afraid of Death? Who, Me?

Through most of my life I felt safe from dying, whether I really was safe or not. Of course, I knew I was mortal and would die sometime, but that "knowing" was theoretical; it had no practical impact on me. Things are now quite different. The cumulative effect of several close calls over a period of years has changed me. Now I feel death threatens, whether it does at the moment or not.

My feelings of vulnerability began to surface about fourteen years ago, soon after my older brother Ron suffered a major heart attack. Ron had been seriously overweight and had suffered from high blood pressure for years. I, by contrast, had none of his indicators for heart trouble. I carried comparatively few excess pounds, exercised regularly, had only borderline high blood pressure and great cholesterol numbers.

One warm summer day while refinishing our garage doors, I began to feel bad—nothing in particular, just a general malaise. I didn't feel I could quit in the middle of the job so I stayed with it. But as soon as I finished, about 5 p.m., I went in to relax. The discomfort continued. I checked my pulse. It was racing at 130 beats per minute in contrast to the usual 70.

I called my doctor, and he ordered me to the emergency room. There they hooked me to a heart monitor, which beeped out an erratic message as my heart skipped beats and continued racing. "We can give you something to slow your heart rate," the young doctor said, "but first we have to be sure you are not having a heart attack." That meant doing an EKG and monitoring my symptoms.

Only then did I begin to think this might be something serious. Even then my possible death was hardly more than a passing thought. Actually, I smiled at the irony of the situation. What if I had a heart attack and died here? After all my concern for Ron and with all my indicators for better heart health, wouldn't it be funny if I died and he lived?

I could be amused at the thought only because I had no real concern it might happen. I was soon diagnosed with paroxysmal atrial tachycardia, which I have since learned is a medical term for rapid heart beat. Now, there was a piece of news! I knew I had rapid heart beat when I went in there. They injected me with verapamil, a calcium channel blocker, and my heart rate quickly returned to normal.

Subsequently, my doctor put me on atenolol, a beta-blocker, and I did well for a long time, with only an occasional minor episode. Then one weekend while I was hiking in the Three Sisters Wilderness area of central Oregon, my rapid pulse returned and would not self-correct. Later in the day, back in the city of Bend, I called the doctor and was again directed to the emergency room.

This visit was much different from the earlier one. At the hospital, my pulse rate suddenly shot up to about 300 beats a minute, and I felt weird and ready to collapse. The doctors frantically engaged in tests and consultations and told me I would need the defibrillator. I'd seen that on TV. They put paddles on your chest and jolt the heart electrically to restore its normal beat.

They administered an amnesiac so I wouldn't remember the otherwise painful jolt. When I awoke I was back to my normal self. They told me the first attempt had failed, but the second was successful.

This heart episode made me feel my life was in danger. I realized that had I not been at the hospital when the fibrillation occurred, I might well have died.

Since nothing else would now control my arrhythmia, my cardiologist put me in the hospital and started me on a regimen of the strongest medicine they had—amiodorone. I tolerated the rather toxic medicine well and have again felt normal for several years. My doctor says there is no reason to think the medicine will lose its effectiveness, and I have no restrictions on my activities. (Maybe I should run for vice president.)

While pursuing one of the "unrestricted activities" the doctor permitted me, I broke my back in a fall from a scaffold. As soon as I hit the ground with a spine-shattering jolt, I checked to see if I still had movement in my arms and legs. Everything worked, and I hobbled to my son Greg's nearby house, but there the pain soon incapacitated me. As for threatening my life, however, that came only after I got to the hospital.

The powerful pain medication they administered left me unable to stay awake. Marj, at my bedside, kept prodding me. "Every time you went to sleep you quit breathing," she told me later. I figure if she hadn't been there to keep me awake—and summon the medical staff to reverse the effects of the medication—I wouldn't be here today.

Taken together, these close-call episodes made me know I was mortal, not just in theory but in fact. I could die!

Now I sometimes go to bed at night not feeling so great and my childhood bedtime prayer takes on new significance: "If I should die before I wake . . ."

Recently I developed a small growth about the size of a paper match head in my right ear. When I tried to surgically remove it with my fingernails, it bled and just got bigger. After wishing it away for three weeks failed, I went to see my doctor. He looked at it for a moment and then said what you never want to hear a doctor say, "Hmm!" He gently poked at it and probed it and again said "Hmm!" Then he added, "I am going to send you to a specialist. It could be a cancer, and I don't feel comfortable removing it myself."

Good night! I thought. *A cancer on my head? What are*

*they going to do if they can't get it all, fry my
brain with radiation?* I knew I wouldn't be
in favor of them removing my whole head.

The specialist didn't have an appointment available for six weeks. I took the
earliest one I could get. Three days later,
I called her office again. "This thing is
growing fast," I explained. "I don't want
to wait six weeks." I got an appointment
for the next Friday.

Meanwhile I reassured myself. Cancer
doesn't run in our family. No one on either
my father's or my mother's side ever had
cancer. *Wait a minute,* I thought, *how
come my mother feared dying of cancer? Did I hear
once that her mother died of cancer? I'm not sure. Hmm.*
What I did know was that my mother died peacefully in
her sleep at age ninety-three—"of causes related to old
age" the death certificate said.

When I got in to see Dr. Redtfeldt (a young woman
who reminded me of my granddaughter Kami), she was
reassuring. "I'll remove it right here in the office. I don't
think it's malignant. We will send it to the pathologist to
make sure. Even if it is malignant, we will get it all, and

it will not come back." Then she told me I'd have to wait ten days or so for the procedure.

Ten more days to "not worry." Then after that, another week before the pathologist's report.

The growth turned out to be benign.

Why Do I Fear Death?

Through most of my life when I had no fear of death, it was for two reasons. First, I had long ago settled the question of my eternal destiny. I had trusted in Christ as my Lord and Savior and received the promise of eternal life. This was no play-it-safe, formal action on my part but a well-considered and heartfelt decision.

The second reason I had no fear was that I never thought seriously about the prospect of my own demise. It was, as I said earlier, just theoretical.

I'd like to say that of these two reasons, my faith in Christ was the principal thing that kept me from fear. But if that were so, why should I be apprehensive now? The only thing that has changed is my sense of mortality. But why should I fear death? Am I not sim-

42

ply going to a better place? That is what I've believed. But that was before I faced the prospect of actually dying. Now I realize there is a lot more I don't know than what I do know about a believer's destiny beyond the veil of death.

We will be reunited with our loved ones (1 Thess 4:16-17), but in what relationship? Will my mother still be my mother? Will my wife and children still be my wife and children? And if not, will they simply be fellow citizens of heaven?

Will we be consciously with the Lord from the moment of death? Or will we sleep until the resurrection, as the sabbath school of my briefly Adventist childhood taught? Will we know what is transpiring on earth? If so, won't our hearts be troubled by the problems of our loved ones? And won't we be devastated by their wrong choices?

I think I know what the Bible says on some of these questions, which is really not that much. But who says my assumptions and interpretations or the confident pronouncements of my teachers are correct?

What finally meant the most to me in all these considerations was the words of Jesus himself. He addressed the question directly:

Do not let your heart be troubled. Trust in God; trust also in me. In my Father's house are many rooms; if it were not so, I would have told you. I am going there to prepare a place for you. And if I go and prepare a place for you, I will come back and take you to be with me that you also may be where I am. (Jn 14:1-3)

My instructors throughout life may have been wrong or right, but Jesus said my expectation of being with him after death is valid. He says I can trust that if it were not valid, he would have said so. I believe I will go from here to be with Jesus in glory, and I believe it on the strength of his personal assurance.

All of this makes me think of the time in my twenties when I had general anesthesia for a tooth extraction. The young woman anesthetist hummed a soothing tune as she held a soft rubber mask over my mouth and nose. Quickly the circle of light shining in my face from the dentist's lamp became smaller. With each breath, the circle shrank, until there was total darkness. *Well, now I'm out,* I thought, but the mask stayed over my face and the darkness grew ever darker. I began to panic. What was wrong with this woman? Didn't she know I was already out? *This woman is trying to kill me,* I thought. *I must hold on!*

Immediately there came a voice closer than hands or feet. "No, I'll hold on to you." I knew it was the Lord. I expect him to be there when it really is time to draw my last breath as well.

I still don't relish the idea of meeting what Scripture calls the last enemy—death. The experience may involve walking through a dark valley. But as David wrote:

Even though I walk
    through the valley of the shadow of death,
I will fear no evil,
    for you are with me. (Ps 23:4)

I think of the three Hebrew young men who were cast alive into a fiery furnace (Dan 3). They actually entered the furnace confident that the Lord would deliver them one way or another—either from the furnace or through it. And he did.

When the world and the devil have done their worst to us, we will emerge from the fire unscathed, just as they did, without even the smell of smoke on us.

What I Want to Be When I Grow Old

I thought I had the forced-retirement problem solved decades before I ever faced it. As a writer, I imagined I was invulnerable.

Two factors force older people out of jobs or careers they want to keep. One is inability to continue doing the work. Had I been a professional athlete, I would have known my years of active competition were limited. Most athletes are "old" by age forty, with a few notable exceptions such as George Foreman.

Workers in almost any field face the same situation as athletes; only the timing is different. Sooner or later the inescapable demands of the job dictate a change. Carpenters get bursitis of the elbow and can no longer swing a hammer. Carpet layers and concrete finishers can't continue to work on their knees. Middle school teachers can't endure the stress of the classroom. Airline pilots can't pass the rigorous physical exams. Surgeons find their hands too unsteady to safely perform delicate operations. Lawyers, police officers, ministers and business executives suffer burnout.

As a writer, however, I thought I would never become too infirm for the job. How much strength does it take to punch a keyboard or put pen to paper?

In addition to disability, the second factor that forces people out of their jobs is age discrimination. Workers who are well able to continue at their jobs are often retired against their will. In the 1990s, corporate loyalty to longtime employees became rare. Cost cutting and competition dictated that corporations replace well-paid older workers with young ones who could be hired for much less. The most cutthroat employers fired older workers shortly before they were due to receive their pensions, leaving them with no job, no prospects of re-hire and no adequate means of support.

I figured I had this one solved too. As a writer I could never be forced out of my job to endure a boring life of meaningless inactivity (or meaningless activity). I could lose my job with a particular publisher, as with any employer, but as a freelancer I could keep writing material that would be published by whoever had the good sense to accept my stuff. I would never be too old since the prospective publisher wouldn't need to know anything about my age.

OUTSMARTING THE FORCED-RETIREMENT SYSTEM

I started writing for publication when I was a pastor about age thirty. For seven years I wrote articles and stories for a wide range of Christian publications, while continuing to be a pastor. By then my writing was well known to Jim Adair, the editor of *Powerline* papers at Scripture Press. He hired me to edit a weekly *Power* paper, and a bit later promoted me to editor of the new book-publishing division, Victor Books.

I liked writing as an occupation because of the broad ministry it offered. It also appealed to me as a career I could continue even when I grew old.

The can't-be-forced-out factor was hugely important to me, partly because of my lifelong aversion to boredom. When I was only eight years old, I was restlessly prowling the house on a lazy summer day. "There's nothing to do," I complained to my mother.

"Nothing to do? You should enjoy your summer vacation while you can. The world is full of interesting things to do. Go out and play with your brother."

"He won't play with me. He thinks I'm too young for him and his friends. It's no fun."

"Well, then, walk down to the library and get some books. You like to read."

That was the first conjunction of two major elements in my life. One, I hated boredom. Two, I liked to read. I learned early, however, that reading was no complete solution to the boredom problem. Once I actually made three trips to the library in one day. Between each trip I went through my small cache of books, reading those I liked and setting aside unread the ones I found boring.

WORSE THAN BOREDOM

I always knew that, for me, forced retirement would be boring, but I learned it could be even worse as a threat to my identity. Years ago Arthur Miller penned a poignant story of just such a situation. In *Death of a Salesman* the main character, Willie Loman (played in the film version by Dustin Hoffman), loses his corporate sales position despite his many years of being "well liked by his customers" (not just liked but well liked, Willie insists). Willie ends up committing suicide, vainly hoping to fulfill with his insurance money his dreams of greatness for his oldest son. Of course, that greatness would have been Willy's vicariously. The son, Biff, who never shared his father's dream for him in the first place, remarked after his father's death, "He never knew who he was."

In a more recent film, *About Schmidt,* Jack Nicholson plays a newly retired insurance executive. Idly surfing channels one day, he comes across an appeal for support for needy children. He responds and soon has a packet introducing him to six-year-old Ndugu, his new foster son in Tanzania.

Urged to write the boy a letter telling about himself, Schmidt takes the opportunity to unload his inner feelings about retirement on this far away little child who has no chance in the world of understanding him. "When I was a kid, I used to think that maybe I was special, that somehow destiny would tap me to be a great man," Schmidt writes. He adds that he had hoped he'd at least be "somebody semi-important."

Schmidt's dreams had never been realized, and now at age sixty-six he had lost what little significance he ever had. Retirement from his job was soon followed by his wife's death, his discovery of a best friend's betrayal and conflict with his grown daughter. After knocking around the country for some time in an RV he and his wife had bought for retirement travels, the pathetic Schmidt returns home to the same forlorn situation he left.

In the stack of mail awaiting him, he finds a letter from Ndugu, written with the help of a nun, the child's caregiver. It thanks God for Schmidt and the difference he is making in the boy's life. The nun says that the boy can't read or write but hopes Schmidt will like the picture he has made for him. The crude artwork shows a big human figure reaching out to touch the outstretched hand of a small one. In the closing scenes of the movie, Schmidt says nothing as he studies the picture, but his tears grow into weeping, and they speak volumes. His life still has validity after all, not in being somebody semi-important but in reaching out and touching one distant little boy.

The ultimate question that confronted me as my writing star faded, which it did despite my best efforts, was the same as faced Loman and Schmidt. Do I know who I am? If so, who? What validity does my life have if I can't pursue my lifelong calling—if I can't do something at least semi-important?

TOO BAD, AND IT WAS SUCH A GOOD PLAN

I didn't want to risk a life of boredom as a retired person, so I followed a career immune to age discrimination. I didn't want to be sidelined from productively serving the Lord, so I chose a vocation I could still pursue when old and infirm.

Just how well did this ingenious plan work out? Well, I still write. Let's see, there was that letter to the insurance company to tell them what I thought of their denial of Marj's auto accident claim. But it went into the circular file, not the mailbox. There are the records I keep so that if I die my survivors will be able to handle my affairs. And there is that journal of sorts, the book my daughter Krystal gave me six years ago, in which I am supposed to write all the pertinent facts of my life (and some of the impertinent ones) for my descendants. Oops, no, I can't count that as writing; it's still blank.

I exaggerate. The book you hold in your hand is evidence of that. In addition, I write a monthly report for

International Christian Writers, a fellowship I direct. I also mentor other writers and critique the writings of still others. I am a publishing consultant to a denominational publication. Nevertheless, the wide open and undiminished opportunity I anticipated has definitely disappeared, even though my abilities haven't. I can rattle off reasons:

1. The law of supply and demand: There are many more good writers now and many fewer good markets for publication than when I started.

2. Lack of drive: After I have published twenty books, I no longer hunger to write for publication so much as I once did.

3. My age: Major book publishers generally prefer to work with authors who have a longer future ahead of them.

4. I am dated: The world moves on, and however vital and relevant I try to be the fact remains that my generation is marching off the stage. New voices are being heard, new writers read. The wisdom that comes with age does count for something, but not enough to balance the scales.

Now what? What else do I want to do? What *can* I do?

LOOKING FOR PLAN B

I have always enjoyed physical work—just not too much of it. Physical work helps keep me fit and provides a welcome break from the mental work of writing. I spent many hours working on cars when I was younger. At some point I figured out that the same effort put into home improvement would be vastly more profitable.

By the time my writing career began to stumble, I had reconditioned a number of houses and built two from the ground up. Now perhaps I could simply adjust the balance of my activity—do more with my home projects and less writing.

One factor made this new plan questionable. My writing has always been explicitly Christian. It serves the Lord. I believed people could read my books and be blessed, built up, encouraged and corrected in their walk with God. That's pretty spiritual and heady stuff compared with, say, painting a room or tiling a cabinet backsplash.

I wrestled with the question of what I should be doing for quite some time. The truth is I felt devalued by doing secular work instead of Christian work. That was ironic because I had written a book in 1988 titled *Take*

This Job and Love It. The book emphasized the biblical teaching that any legitimate work done for Christ is fully accepted by him and will be fully rewarded, even if it's slave labor (Col 3:22-24). I knew that was true, but it didn't fix me. I reasoned that secular work was fine for others, but I was called to Christian work. That must be why I still felt compromised.

The apostle Paul was a tentmaker so you can do secular work too, I told myself.

Yes, but he didn't make tents to make tents; he only did it to support himself so that he could preach the gospel, I replied.

Eventually I found the most help for my dilemma by looking at Jesus himself. He spent most of his working life as a carpenter. He was thirty years old before he ever started to preach, and he preached for only three years. Why did such a man "waste" his time making perishable items of wood for so long? I couldn't have done that and still have felt I was fulfilling the will of God for my life.

My commitment to serve Christ went back to my middle teen years. I sang bass in a male quartet, and one of our songs was "I Want My Life to Tell for Jesus." I had no idea my life could tell *for* Jesus without my vocation telling *about* him.

I figured worldly work would have no heavenly reward. A popular saying in our church was:

Only one life, 'twill soon be past;
Only what's done for Christ will last.

But looking at Jesus now, in the midst of an identity crisis of sorts, I was surprised to discover that the Father's endorsement of him came before he started preaching and while he was still a carpenter. He had done no miracles, preached no sermons, healed no one, cast out no demons. At about age thirty he went down to the river Jordan to be baptized by John. As he came up out of the water, the Father spoke from heaven, "This is my Son, whom I love; with him I am well pleased" (Mt 3:17).

This insight hit me with the force of a divine revelation. I realized that I had misinterpreted the admonitions about devoting our life to Christ's service. I thought it had to do with *what we do.* I learned it has more to do with *how* and *why* we do it, whatever it is.

This was a tremendous help because it elevated all

my work and made it all an instrument of fulfillment and meaning in my life. I could paint that room or tile that backsplash for Jesus and know he would accept my work for him. I recalled that he always valued service to others above all else, and my home improvements were definitely a service to the people who would live in that home for years to come.

I think of the long, difficult struggle my friend Carol Wilkinson had when she and her husband, Ted, were threatened by age and health issues with the termination of their lifelong mission to Japan. Painfully, Carol came to see that she is not a missionary to Japan. Rather, she is a Christian doing missionary work in Japan. When she can no longer do that, she will be a Christian serving God in some other way, at some other place.

I don't want to be smug about what I see as my successful struggle with age-related career change. Not all career change is solved by realizing we can serve Christ in whatever work we perform. The day may come when we can do no productive work at all.

An endearing image from an earlier generation has Grandpa sitting on a rocker on the front porch whittling. Or Grandma sitting there knitting. Even now, I would probably have a spiritual struggle with restrictions on my work as severe as that.

Yet I believe that God's grace is sufficient for that as well. Already I have an inkling of what the process may be. Whether whittling or knitting, we can do it unto the Lord and take pride in the work. These activities can and do produce works of art. Not museum quality, perhaps, but works of art nevertheless. How many artists spend their entire lives creating art that never makes the important galleries?

If I end up spending my last years working at something as nonutil-itarian as art, I can find fulfillment in it. And if I can't even do that, I can still serve the basic purpose I was created for—to worship God. The same grace and leading of God's Spirit that transformed my "exile" from my former career into a sense of purpose and fulfillment will be with me then too. For I have learned that I am not a writer; I am a Christian who writes.

I Can Change and I'll Prove It

A few years ago a dreadful thing happened to margarine. It was quietly, almost surreptitiously, replaced by something called "spread." The same brand names and essentially the same packaging cloaked a quite different product.

I didn't even know there had been a change until I innocently slathered some of this new "spread" on my toast. I put it to my mouth and found the toast was *all wet*. What was this? I checked the package and soon figured out that this product was not margarine but a reduced-fat spread. And how was this reduction in fat obtained? By mixing in water. It disgusted me that they had watered down my product with no notice and no corresponding reduction in price. Worse, I hated wet toast.

PLEASE PASS THE BUTTER

When I was growing up, we seldom had anything but margarine for our bread and toast. We called it oleo. It came in a one-pound bar (no cubes, no tubs), and it was white like lard. A small yellow packet cowered like contraband somewhere in the package. To change the unappetizing white color of oleo to a buttery yellow, consumers had to knead the two products together.

We knew what butter was. We enjoyed its wonderful rich flavor on special occasions, but it was too expensive for daily use. This situation continued after I married and had my own family. Later, we also began to hear that animal fats were bad for us, adding another strike against butter.

In due time margarine, the sensible solution, came under attack as being itself unhealthy. Those hydrogenated fats were as bad for us as butter. I began to get a bit skeptical about warnings against various foods. What the "it's bad for you" folks recommended one year, they cautioned against the next. I decided that moderation was the first rule, and favoring natural foods was second. That second principle meant no artificial sweeteners, and butter would be better than margarine. If I could afford it.

Then came that "spread" fiasco, foisted on me without so much as a please or thank you. I decided I had denied myself butter long enough, and a change was due. We *could* afford butter now. It wasn't *that* expensive, and we didn't use that much of it. As for consuming too much animal fat, that seemed unlikely. Red meat had been an entrée on our dinner table only modestly more often than butter was our spread. Yesterday's self-denial was fine, but now it was payoff time. "Please pass the butter."

TIME FOR DESSERT

Deciding in favor of butter was a small thing, but it involved a significant change in my thinking, because forgoing butter was part of a larger package. When I was growing up, my folks enforced a strict rule at our dinner table—no dessert until we had finished our dinners. It was a good rule and translated readily into other good principles, such as "work before pleasure." Both rules fostered the self-discipline necessary to success in life.

After "spread" made its ugly appearance, however, the permission I gave myself to use butter was accompanied by the realization that I *had* eaten my dinner. It was time for dessert. Forever delaying dessert would mean never enjoying it at all. That seemed hardly what our loving heavenly Father had in mind. In fact, it made no sense. The obvious had at last penetrated my mind: What's appropriate for one stage or circumstance of life isn't necessarily appropriate for another.

This new thinking soon enabled me to initiate other changes on similar principles.

The fiftieth anniversary of our marriage was approaching, and I wanted to do something special for Marj. A trip wasn't a good idea; she doesn't really like to travel and had chased around the planet with me quite enough already, thank you. I could take her to a country music concert the next time one of our favorite artists came to Portland. She would like that, yes, but it hardly seemed enough.

At last an idea found me. I would take her to a concert or a live play once every month throughout our anniversary year. Checking schedules for coming events, I discovered the idea was going to work out well. The Statler Brothers were coming to town soon, and they would perform at the Schnitzer, one of the best concert venues in our city. With light heart and high hopes I went to the nearest outlet to buy tickets. That's when the downside of implementing my plan struck me squarely in the face. The tickets were expensive! However, they did have some seats in the third balcony—the nosebleed section—for less than a third the cost of good seats toward the front of the main floor.

Please understand that my mind was conditioned by long years of choosing margarine over butter. *What? They expect me to pay a huge premium for better seats at the same event? Fat chance!* The ticket agent sensed my reluctance. "I can't guarantee that these better seats, or any seats, will be available later," he said. I nodded, mumbled something meaningless and walked away from the ticket office empty-handed.

What to do, what to do? Obviously if we were going to attend, I had to make some decision soon. My rational mind took over. *When in doubt, analyze your options.*

1. You can pay these outlandish prices and buy the good seats. *(But will your frugal side ever forgive you?)*

2. You can buy the cheaper seats. Marj probably won't complain. Hey, at least she gets to be there. But is that the big celebration you want to give her? Is this the time to be cheap?

3. You can forget about this every-month idea altogether. *(Oh, sure, after you've already told her.)*

4. You can buy her a ticket for a good seat and one for yourself in the balcony. *(OK, this is the time to consider all options, but that one's really nutty.)*

I went against all my instincts from younger years and bought the good seats, two of them. My next test followed the night of the concert. Could I enjoy the Statler Brothers without sitting there miffed the whole time over the high prices I had paid?

I needn't have worried. What a night it was! We were close enough to see the dots on bass singer Harold Reid's tie, and we loved every minute of it. I also felt good that for once I had bought Marj something nice, without even getting a discount. And I had proved to myself that I could change. That in itself was a nice payoff.

I'm still a man who looks for value for every cent I

spend. No doubt I will always be that way. But I'm learning there's more than one way to measure value. I have been consistently more generous since switching to butter and buying the good seats at the Statler Brothers concert, and I am sure that's a change for the better.

Some time ago Marj and I were talking with our grown granddaughter Heidi. The subject of her childhood memories came up, and she thought of her Uncle Dave, always one of the more generous of our family members. "He gave me the happiest fun time of my entire childhood," she recalled. "He took his kids—Josh and Bridgette and Ben—and us three kids—Lora and Kami and me—up to Mt. Hood, and he paid for all of us to ride the snow slides. I couldn't believe it. It was soooo fun, and I'll never forget his generosity."

I don't know what that outing cost Dave, but I know I wouldn't have spent it. Now I'm thinking he chose the better way, and I . . . well, it's a pity. But at least now my changed outlook can save what's left of the day.

Cutting Back

People sometimes need to tighten their purse strings rather than loosen them as they grow older. They must change in an opposite direction from me. People find their pensions disappearing, their investments going sour, their finances devastated by unforeseen disasters. More than one member of our extended family enjoyed butter and better seats for years, only to find they didn't have the resources to maintain that lifestyle later in life.

My brother Ron and I were polar opposites in this regard. He always lived well, spent freely and, to his credit, was generous toward others. One time he took our entire extended family out for an expensive lobster dinner. No occasion; he just wanted to do it.

Marj and I laugh about our feeble attempts to reciprocate. Once we found a real bargain advertised in the local paper and seized on the opportunity to invite Ron *and* his wife Shirley to lunch— on us. I have to admit that garden salad special at Kmart was not that great.

Ron came on hard times later in life. He took early retirement from his position as president of *Parents* Magazine's Cultural Institute (PMCI) and moved from his Westport, Connecticut, mansion back to his birth state of Oregon. Here he maintained a home in Portland, and he also kept a much-loved lakeside retreat at Twin Lakes, Idaho. Despite a greatly reduced income, he continued to live on butter.

When disposable funds ran short at one point, he still ate butter but let his health coverage lapse briefly. About that time he suffered a major heart attack, at which point he became uninsurable. The cost of his open-heart surgery and other treatments ruined him financially. He didn't look for a bridge to jump from, however. He changed, drastically curtailed his spending, and wasn't too proud to be on the receiving end of others' generosity when they offered it. He did manage to keep his lakeside retreat, where four years later he passed away of his third heart attack.

Older people (and all people for that matter) need to be able to change with changing circumstances, whether that means to spend more freely or to turn frugal. Like the apostle Paul, we need to be able to say, "I know what it is to be in need, and I know what it is to have plenty" (Phil 4:12). Paul could change according to the circumstances he faced.

WHY CHANGE COMES HARD

Finances are only one area where we may need to

change as we age. Styles change in everything, and standards change as well. If we don't change, we simply will be left behind.

A chief reason older people are unable to accommodate change, much less initiate it, is that we often see change as bad or, at best, unnecessary. Others may say we are "set in our ways," but we honestly think the old ways are better. "If it's not broke, don't fix it," we say, settling the question with unassailable logic. Jesus commented on this kind of thinking. He said, "No one after drinking old wine, wants the new, for he says, 'The old is better'" (Lk 5:39).

For me, a critical element in being able to change is seeing that the old very well may not be better, not now, given all the circumstances of my life. I must recognize that my preference for the old ways may be totally subjective. I think the old ways are better because I am comfortable with them. Recognizing that, I must deliberately choose to be open-minded on these questions.

I like country music—traditional country music, not the loud, noisy stuff that passes for country music today. But that noisy stuff is not intrinsically inferior; it just seems that way to me. Similarly, many of my contemporaries like the old hymns better than today's worship choruses. But though they can make plausible arguments for the superiority of hymns, I find their arguments unconvincing and their indignation unjustified. I suspect what is really happening is that they are married to the status quo, don't like the new ways, and therefore find reasons to support their preferences.

When I was a pastor, I once had on my desktop a cartoon. Rear engine cars such as the Volkswagen and the Corvair were just coming into general use. The cartoon showed a salesman with a customer, surveying the rear-located engine. The customer doesn't like the change at all. "I think engines should be in the front," he says, "the way God intended."

My surprise came when a member visited me in my study one day, looked over the cartoon and said in all seriousness, "That's right. I feel the exact same way."

It's OK, I think, to "feel the exact same way" about morally neutral changes that confront us, just so long as we recognize that it really is a *feeling* we are talking about. And we *can* change whether we feel like it or not.

When I Can No Longer Do Good Stuff, Like Drive

I am a safe driver. Most of those who once were afraid to ride with me can do so fully relaxed now, most of the time. You must understand that I'm used to the steep, winding, mountain roads of the West. Those who aren't so conditioned may think I drive such dangerous roads much too fast. Not so. Hey, it keeps me awake.

I wasn't always a safe driver. One of my first driving experiences nearly killed us all—my brother Ron, sister Levauna, mother and me. Ron and I were working for the summer washing dishes at Levauna's restaurant in central

California. Mom had come down to visit. Ron had been taking me out on back-country roads in Levauna's car and teaching me to drive, despite the fact that he was underaged and unlicensed, and I was only twelve.

This time Mom and Levauna were with us. Ron had taught me to make "California stops" at stop signs. One slows to a roll while looking to see if there is any traffic coming on the crossroad. As we approached a large X-shaped sign, Ron said to stop for the railroad crossing. I implemented my "California stop" procedure as I rolled near the tracks.

I neither saw nor heard the approaching train. "Stop, there's a train coming!" Mom yelled. I hit the brakes. "Go," yelled Ron, "you're already on the tracks!"

I hit the accelerator, but the car was in third gear and had no accelerating power. As we lurched across the track, I looked to my left and saw the engine bearing down on us. About that time Mom grabbed the steering wheel and jerked it to the right. We plunged off the road, careened off an embankment, bounced back and came to rest crosswise on the road just beyond the train tracks. I didn't drive again for three years.

When I did start driving, the mothers of the girls at church wouldn't let them ride with me. I was a perfectly able driver, but just because I "dug out," spinning my wheels and throwing gravel when I left one of their homes, they discriminated against me.

I admit I also had a few accidents. In fact, there was one particularly sharp curve that I failed to negotiate two different times, ending up in the ditch. That may sound bad, but, hey, I was going in opposite directions on those two occasions. How was I to know the curve was just as sharp either way?

A good many years have passed since I last had an auto accident, but my driving was nevertheless suspended relatively recently. Not by the authorities but by disability.

In 2001 I broke my back in a fall from a scaffold. My recovery took a long time, and at first I was totally dependent. Once I was stabilized, the hospital nurse had to teach me how to roll over in bed. "Like a log," she said, meaning, I gathered, that I wasn't to flex my spine at all. It wasn't easy, and I never was sure I was doing it right. All I knew was that it hurt, no matter how I did it.

Eventually I was released, still totally

dependent and also totally glad to be out of that place and into the familiar scenes of home. As I progressed, I was able at last to sleep without the confining body "corset" I'd been wearing around the clock. Each morning before I could get up, Marj had to belt me into it again.

Before long, to the surprise of everyone, I returned to church and to the adult class I was teaching. Of course, Marj had to help me into the car and drive me there. A friend, Don McLaughlin, met us in the parking lot with a wheelchair. He wheeled me into the church, then into the elevator and down to my class.

All through my recuperation, everybody was more than accommodating, including Marj, who bore the full brunt of my disability. She never complained, but I knew full well it couldn't be any fun.

The saving element in the ordeal was hope. I never doubted that my disability was temporary. My neurosurgeon, a Christian and an instructor at Oregon Health Sciences University, said I would slowly improve for a full year. Any disability or pain I still had after a year was with me for good.

Meanwhile, I was getting a firsthand lesson in how demeaning it can feel to be disabled. I had always been the provider, protector and problem-fixer for Marj. Now I was a burden.

Happily, those days are behind us. After one year I was able to tell the many supportive friends who inquired that I was "almost totally back to abnormal."

DISABILITY TAKES MANY FORMS

While my back is remarkably restored, I notice the number of unrelated things I can no longer do is growing. I say "can no longer do," but it would be more accurate to say I can no longer *enjoy* doing them. The price I must pay to do them is more than they are worth to me.

For example, I can no longer enjoy being out past ten at night. I have always been a morning person, but my coach is turning into a pumpkin earlier all the time. It scares me a bit because I remember my mother. Her days got shorter and shorter, and toward the end she was preparing for bed at four in the afternoon.

Taking intercontinental trips is another lost function. In 2002 I had to announce reluctantly that I could not continue to take such flights—some involving thirty hours elapsed time or even more—to far-off parts of the world to help train Christian writers. I could still direct

International Christian Writers, but I could no longer meet the rigorous travel demands of going personally.

About the same time I had to call a halt to my fishing excursions. My longtime fishing buddy, Glen Thornton, and I had made weeklong trips to eastern Oregon desert reservoirs once or twice a year, almost forever it seemed. The last time we planned to go, I was fixing up Glen's RV while he and his wife, Nancy, were wintering in Arizona. I was doing the work, and he was footing the bill. After all that, we ended up not going for some reason I don't recall. Nancy said, "It was so funny; neither of you really wanted to go."

Inwardly, I had to admit she spoke the truth. Of course, in my case, I had good reason. Medication I was taking made me extremely sun sensitive, and I suffered out in our open boat. As for Glen, well, I guess he was just getting soft.

We had Glen and Nancy over for games just the other evening. Glen and I agreed that come spring, we'll likely go fishing again. Nancy didn't say a word.

DISABLED, DEPENDENT AND DISAGREEABLE?

My friend and new colleague, Clyde Cowan, is one of those who has taken up the task of traveling to far-off places to teach Christian writers. Clyde has worked in twenty-eight countries as a specialist in crosscultural ministries. In 2000 he was stricken with Graves Disease. It left him unable to see clearly and sometimes even to think clearly. For eighteen months his wife, Paula, became his driver as he sought to continue his ministry as much as possible, at least in the United States.

For Clyde, being unable to drive was a disaster. He wrote about his driving issues with Paula in a piece he called "Driving Mrs. Daisy Crazy." Many men are critical of their wife's driving, even minus a vision impairment that made it appear to Clyde that Paula was about to collide with a pedestrian or another car.

One day his criticism got to be too much for Paula. She pulled to the side of the road and said through tears that she would not drive him anymore. Though they were on the way to an important meeting, she turned the car around and drove home, ignoring both his demands and his contrition. "Call a cab," she told him.

With Paula refusing to drive him again, Clyde became desperate about his need to control his reactions. "I knew that much of it was simply frustration at my condition, displaced on the nearest 'safe' objects—other drivers oblivious to my angry words, and my longsuffering wife. My face flushes now with shame for the hurt I caused her."

Paula did finally relent and drove him again. With iron discipline bolstered by his love for his wife, whom he didn't want to hurt, Clyde made it through a day without saying a word about her driving. "Two days, three—I worked myself all the way to day 22," writes Clyde. "On the 23rd day Paula pulled into a parking spot, and confronted me for criticizing the way she parked. 'I didn't say a word,' I protested. 'You flinched,' she said, 'and body language counts.'"

IT GETS WORSE

In Clyde's experience, as in mine, the dependence was temporary. For some people it is for the rest of their lives. That seems like one of the hardest scenarios I can imagine, for both the disabled person and the caregiver. Yet I believe the Lord can and does redeem even that worst situation.

I remember how awed I was years ago when Dr. Robert McQuilken, president of Columbia Bible College, resigned his post to devote his life to caring for his wife, who had a debilitating disease. To me, it seemed he went from a great ministry for the Lord with worldwide implications to being caregiver for one sick woman.

Of course he should provide for her care, I thought, *but he wouldn't have to care for her himself. Surely he could hire someone for that task and continue his great ministry.* Evidently for Dr. McQuilkin, though, it wasn't a *task* but a life partner needing his love and care.

Though I couldn't understand his choice at the time, somewhere deep inside I knew he had done an unusually noble thing. It was the kind of noble thing for which Mother Teresa was later to be acclaimed around the world. She gave herself for those who were dying alone and forgotten on the streets of Calcutta, though they were totally unable to do anything for her in return.

If I implicitly admire those who care for the helpless, Jesus was explicit about it. He said, "The greatest among you will be your servant" (Mt 23:11). He also said, "I was sick and you looked after me. . . . I tell you the truth, whatever you did for one of the least of these brothers of mine, you did for me" (Mt 25:36, 40).

It's a good thing he said what he did. If he hadn't, imagine how much less care there would be for the helpless and how much more unrelieved suffering. Some no doubt serve the helpless without regard to Christ's admonition. But great works of compassion have grown out of the church for centuries because Christ commanded it.

Unlike Mother Teresa, most people who give themselves to the care of the helpless never receive any applause. But Jesus said that many who are last here will be first in the kingdom to come. I can't think of anyone to whom those words better apply than to those who have sacrificed their own interests to care for others.

Jesus redeems our disabilities. He honors those who care for the disabled, thus redeeming their service. But that couldn't happen if there were no disabled. So they too can find redemption in their suffering, enduring it patiently for the Lord rather than complaining, being demanding and generally making things harder. And if, by the grace of God, they are recipients of tender care, they will have received one of life's greatest gifts—the knowledge that they are truly loved.

Thanks, Marj.

Left Behind
by Those I Loved

She was my big sister—and much more than that.
Levauna was ten years older than I and in many ways
like a second mother. It was she who gave me my first
paying job when I was nine. She paid me ten cents a
day to come and make her bed and straighten up her
apartment.

When my parents gave me a twenty-five-cent toy car
for my tenth birthday, she gave me my very own $7 ta-
ble radio so I could listen to Rollie Truett call the Portland Beavers baseball game.

She told me jokes, helped me solve riddles and
played games that taught me more than school ever did.

She drilled me on the names of the states and capitals, and told about her own travels to "far away places." (Having never been out of the community where I was born, any place seemed far away to me.) She asked me who first sailed around the world (Magellan) and who sought the fountain of youth and found Florida (Ponce de León).

She taught me the parts of speech and the meaning of new words. And she made it all fun.

When I turned sixteen and needed a car but couldn't afford one, she went in with me and we bought it together. She introduced me to Chinese food, which she made herself. At Christmas she whipped up soapsuds and created our family's first flocked tree. She made fudge and divinity and penuche, and even tried hand-dipped chocolates once.

When I married and went to Bible college, she let Marj and me live rent free in the small house behind the big one she and her husband, Smitty, had by then. Later, they got a summer cabin near North Twin Lake in central Oregon and invited our family to vacation there.

I don't mean that Levauna was saintly. In her mid-twenties she did time in an Iowa reformatory for mugging a guy she met in a tavern. She was sometimes vulgar and always headstrong. She knew nothing of finesse or tact. But she was my sister, and I loved her. I loved her because I knew she loved me. She made me feel she always would, no matter what.

Even into my own middle age, Levauna was my support. She bought, read, praised and distributed my books. If I was in any trouble, she let me know she was there to help.

When I was sixty-four years old, Levauna died, and I became an "orphan." My father had died when I was ten. My mother still lived but was more like my child than my mother. But Levauna! I felt diminished when my older brother Ron died a couple of years before. And now I was diminished again, only more.

Some time after her death, I was going through Levauna's effects and found my own earliest writings. She had saved the letters I wrote her as a child, when I still lived in Bend, Oregon, and she had gone to a far-off place a hundred miles away with the romantic sounding name, Cottage Grove.

They say that the child is father of the man, and it was clear from those letters that was the case with me. At age eleven I was writing her long, newsy letters. I told her at length how I allocated for various purposes the proceeds from my newspaper route. The smallest sum went for entertainment, more for clothing and the largest for savings. I was also able to tell her that strawberries were three boxes for nineteen cents, on special.

I told her I was participating in a reading contest at the library, the winner to be announced on KBND, the new and only radio station in our town. Later I had to backtrack and write, "They won't let me join that contest I told you about, because I read murder mysteries." My selections at the time: the writings of Ellery Queen and of Erle Stanley Gardiner.

In my letters I kept Levauna fully informed of family developments, including news of extended family such as Aunt Sylvia and Uncle Roy on their forty-acre farm. I'd always loved that farm. There were places to roam, things to see, animals to watch, even a pond full of goldfish big as a man's hand.

In one of my letters to Levauna I gave her sad news from Aunt Sylvia's farm: "Sylvia got kicked down and kicked a couple more times and then trampled all over by a cow." Later, the same letter said (even more sad to me), "Sylvia is trying to sell her place and all the stock and everything for $5,000." Evidently I saw no connection between being cow-kicked and selling because my next sentence was: "She says the work is too hard on Roy."

LOOKING AHEAD

Older people are sometimes dismissed as "living in the past." Maybe some of them are. Maybe it sounds like I am. I don't think so. And I wouldn't make that judgment so easily about others either.

I am probably more future-oriented than I have ever been in my life. It's just that my future lies on the other side of the veil. So does yours. Whether you are twenty or forty or one hundred, your future lies on the other side. That's where you will spend eternity after this short earthly journey is over.

I figure it will be great. I may not know much about it, but I do know some things. When Christ returns, both the dead in Christ and those still living will be "caught up together" to "meet the Lord in the air. And so we will be with the Lord forever" (1 Thess 4:17).

I take encouragement in those words, just as the next verse says I should. It's not that I no longer have anyone here and must look to heaven to be with loved ones. Marj and I have five children with families of their own, and we love them dearly. We love our friends, some of recent acquaintance and some we've known for fifty years. But they don't replace parents—or parent figures like Levauna. I hope some day after I'm gone my orphaned children will look forward to being reunited with me. I hope they will remember me fondly and sometimes get a lump in their throats as they recall moments from the life we have shared.

If they do, I hope they won't be living in the past but in the future. And it is nothing short of wonderful that God says that future will come. In fact Christianity itself is intrinsically future-oriented in this same way. That's what the cross is all about. Jesus endured the cross "for the joy set before him," the joy of our eternal gathering with him and with those who have gone on before us (Heb 12:2). Then will be answered Jesus' prayer: "Father, I want those you have given me to be with me where I am, and to see my glory" (Jn 17:24).

Meanwhile, I can hardly imagine what it will be like if I outlive Marj. When she goes away for only a few days, I flounder and lose my bearings. It's not that I can't take care of myself. I can. But why? What's the use? Everything seems to go flat and lose its purpose.

It seems as if, at that time, I would have only two choices. Find another life partner or die.

Once I would probably have rejected such thinking. Life goes on. We never give up and we never give in. But I now suspect there comes a time when a person is ready to move on, when our contemporaries are mostly on the other side, when we are tired and homesick for heaven.

I'm not there yet. Hope not to be there any time soon. But I can conceive of such a thing now. And from here, it doesn't look as defeatist and unspiritual as it once did.

I don't see my physical life here on this planet as something to hold on to at any cost. These days, people's lives are extended by medical science long after they would otherwise have died. I might be one of those people, and I'm still very much glad to be here, so I'm not knocking medical science. But to be kept alive by extraordinary means, in pain and with no hope of recovery? That makes no sense to one who has finished his course and is ready for heaven. But it happens because doctors aren't allowed to take it upon themselves to "pull the plug." That's why, years ago already, I signed a living will directing that no such extraordinary measures be taken.

The apostle Paul came to a time when he felt he was ready to go. Late in life he wrote to Timothy, "The time has come for my departure. I have fought the good fight, I have finished the race, I have kept the faith. Now there is in store for me the *crown of righteousness*, which the Lord, the righteous Judge, will award to me on that day" (2 Tim 4:7-8, italics added).

I don't see that crown as being a metal headpiece. No, like Paul, we will be crowned *with righteousness*. We will finally receive the complete personal righteousness that we have only seen afar off until now. And that righteousness will be bestowed on us by "the righteous Judge." In these words we hear echoes of the grace message Paul preached all through his ministry: Because of Christ's atonement God can be both "just and the one who justifies those who have faith in Jesus" (Rom 3:26).

Receiving a crown, being reunited with loved ones,

experiencing what it really means, finally, to be without flaw or blemish—that's my future. That's even better than the brightest days of the past. What's more, I'll never feel like an orphan again.

I Want to Finish Well

My style is to analyze everything, including my own writing. Rumor has it that I carry analytical thinking to a fault. A few friends over the years have told me directly, "You think too much." I figure if a few said it, others probably think it.

Hmm, maybe I do think too much. I will have to analyze the criticism to determine whether it is valid.

Yes, yes, I know, there I go, doing it again.

In my defense, though, doesn't the Bible say to analyze everything, especially our own lives? "The unexamined life is not worth living." Oops! I guess that was Plato, not the Bible. But it's a good line. Of course, a person can carry self-analysis too far. Life is to be lived, not constantly dissected and examined. As one wag put it, reversing Plato, "The unlived life is not worth examining."

At this point in my life analyzing it means figuring out how to finish well. That isn't a given. It's one thing to go to heaven and quite another to experience a glorious entrance there. The Bible talks about some who are saved "but only as one escaping through the flames," their hoped-for rewards all burned up (see 1 Cor 3:15).

I don't want to just barely make it in. I want, as Peter wrote, to "receive a rich welcome into the eternal kingdom of our Lord and Savior Jesus Christ" (2 Pet 1:11). I want to sail from these waters into eternity with flags unfurled.

That's not just an expression. Flags serve two major purposes on ships. They identify the vessel with its country, and they communicate messages. A furled flag is one that's wrapped or rolled tightly rather than being displayed. I want my vessel to bear the unfurled flag that declares I belong to Christ's kingdom. I want my message flags flying as well, especially the one that signals the Captain is on board.

To me, that means I must hold fast to the great principles that have guided my life to this point and not turn from them when I am old. The danger is that I may. Some do.

For example, is old age a time to replace self-control with self-indulgence? I don't think so, since self-control is a fruit of the Spirit, not an optional lifestyle. I wrote earlier about replacing margarine with butter on our table. I wrote about buying better seats at a concert instead of the cheapest. I concluded that for me such actions were appropriate and were an expression of faith, not its abandonment. That choice of butter and better seats doesn't mean I now embrace pleasure as the focus of my life in its declining years.

As always, it's a matter of seeking the right balance.

I don't want to be the man Job described, who "dies in bitterness of soul, never having enjoyed anything good" (Job 21:25). But neither do I want to forget that, as Paul wrote, "The widow who lives for pleasure is dead even while she lives" (1 Tim 5:6). You see, a widow could take the attitude that she has served her time. Now, with no husband to accommodate and no children to rear, she can just have fun. Rather like some people view retirement.

But Scripture says, "Always give yourselves fully to the work of the Lord, because you know that your labor in the Lord is not in vain" (1 Cor 15:58). I don't think that "always" expires on one's sixty-fifth birthday, or ninety-fifth for that matter.

One aspect of giving myself fully to the work of the Lord involves specific services I can render. Another aspect consists of continuing the good fight of faith that began when I first brought my ship under command of the Lord Jesus Christ.

There are two specific ministries I can provide *only because I am older.*

I Can Be a Mentor

I was fortunate enough to have a mentor for my writing career. Jim Adair was the original longtime editor of *Power* papers at Scripture Press. When he hired me to edit the teen paper, *Power Life,* he became my mentor.

I thought I was a good writer already. I had sold dozens of stories and articles to a whole range of periodicals during the seven years after I began writing for publication. Didn't that prove I was good? Furthermore, Jim Adair had hired me on the strength of the many stories I had written for *Power.*

My first month on the job, I learned how much I didn't know. No one had ever actually gone over my work line by line, word by word, and then sat with me to explain how to make it better. Of course, Jim wasn't always right—he was right only about 90 percent of the time.

Since those years I have had occasion to mentor some other writers, but for the most part I have concentrated on my own writing. Sometimes I have been a bit smug about that choice and dismissive of teaching others. "Those who can (write) do, and those who can't (write) teach."

In later years, however, I have done more mentoring. In some ways teaching others to write well is a greater service than doing it myself. I am only one, my capacity at best is limited, but I can help equip many— not to be my clones, certainly, but to best develop and use their own unique gifts and insights. I will pass away, but they will live on for many more years. There is also less danger that I am acting out of ego-centered motives when I stay in the background and get no byline or recognition.

Mentoring also includes teaching life skills other than writing. I've been teaching money management and personal resourcefulness and good judgment to my children and grandchildren, mainly by example. Sometimes they don't think I am right. Eventually, they decide that I am about 90 percent of the time.

It's gratifying to have them come to me for advice. That is altogether different—and better—than for me to preach at them.

I CAN CONFER A BLESSING

When I was a teenager, I went with my buddy Bill Smith to a home where his Uncle Percy lay dying. I waited in the car while Bill went in for a brief visit. Uncle Percy had called for Bill, as it turned out, to bless Bill from his deathbed. He spoke of Bill's promising future if he faithfully followed the Lord, and then he prayed for him.

When Bill came out, I could tell he was moved. So was I. What a wonderful thing to have a godly elder care about your spiritual welfare and pray specifically for you. I envied him such a heritage.

I have five children and thirteen grandchildren. I'd like to bless them, much like the Old Testament patriarchs blessed their children. I have no guarantee, of course, that I will lie on a deathbed long enough and lucid enough to make that possible. I also don't know what I would say. For a "word guy," I am certainly at a loss for words sometimes, especially when the situation is an emotional one.

Maybe I will have to write out my blessing and file it away for them to read after I am gone. I'm not sure that's quite the same, but it would be something. Or I could write it and give it to them now. I must analyze those options.

Continuing the Good Fight of Faith

I wrote earlier in this chapter that I can obey the biblical admonition to always give myself fully to the work of the Lord, both by rendering age-enabled services *and* by continuing the good fight of faith.

As the expression says, the life of faith is a fight. An unseen battle rages between the kingdom of God and the minions of Satan. While fighting that battle is not unique to old age, it's also true that I can never retire from it, because Satan's minions won't let me. They are on the attack, and I have to be ready to fight back or I am at their mercy, of which they have none.

"Against what temptations does an old guy like you still have to fight?" someone may ask. My answer: almost everything I face daily carries potential for victory or defeat. For example, there's my physical state. Recently I have had a bout with extremely high blood pressure readings late at night. Do I call the doctor after hours? Go to the emergency room? Double up on my medicines? Trust the Lord and forget about it? Pray? Calm my heart and mind by meditating on Scripture? Tell Marj? Don't tell Marj?

Whatever I do involves struggle on my part. I must sort out all these options and possible combinations. I should trust the Lord, of course. He also expects me to use whatever means are at my disposal to deal with the problem. Maybe he has made me aware of the high numbers so I can do something. But what? If I call my doctor after hours, will he think me a hypochondriac? Will he say to take two aspirin and call him in the morning? One night I did call and got the doctor standing in for mine, and that's about what he said. His parting words didn't do a lot to relieve my concern. "Good luck."

Good luck? *Good luck!* I was hoping for something a bit more substantial.

Suppose, however, that instead of having an acute health concern, I feel great. My numbers are all normal, and I feel like my younger self. I am grateful, of course, and tell the Lord as much. This continues for, oh, say, about three days in a row. By then I find myself already taking my health for granted. I feel good? I am *supposed* to feel good.

Then comes an inner accusation. "You miserable ingrate. You should be on your face. You have no guarantees, you know. You had better be more grateful or the Lord may withdraw this blessing that you so obviously don't appreciate."

Then a still small voice tells me the Lord doesn't feel that way at all. I don't have to earn his blessing by showing a certain amount of gratitude. Good health is God's norm for man. It is a state properly taken for granted because it is *granted*—it is the free gift of a loving God, who is pleased that I enjoy it.

Battle won.

PEACE OF MIND

Much of my "good fight of faith" these days relates to Satan's attempts to destroy my peace, as I have just described. I guess he has no peace himself and doesn't want me to have any either. One way he tries to rob me of peace is through premonitions of disaster.

I have flown into Portland International Airport on many occasions. One was unlike any other. The big DC10 approached its landing normally. We were flying blind through heavy cloud cover, but that was not unusual. Shortly we would break through and see the gorgeous greens and browns of my home state, Oregon—the most beautiful place on earth. Still, I was a wee bit nervous. The cloudbank seemed unusually deep, the blind-flying-time long.

Then we broke through, much closer to the ground than I had ever seen before. The engines abruptly roared and we began climbing. They sounded strong, normal, powerful. As we gained altitude, it was apparent that we were going around for another approach. Great, but there was still just as much cloud cover. Why would this attempt be any better than the first one? All this time there wasn't a word from the captain. No assurances that all was well, no explanations—nothing. I had a premonition. I could hear the news report. "DC10 crashes on approach to Portland International Airport, no survivors."

On our second approach the pilot somehow found a

much better channel through the cloud cover and we landed normally.

Obviously my premonition was not an evidence of something actually about to happen. I had experienced premonitions before. Not about something so cataclysmic, but, for example, about a late-arriving loved one having had an auto accident. After the situations passed, I quickly forgot the premonitions. Now I wondered. Were any of these premonitions valid? I decided to check it out. I would make it a point to notice whether any of the things I anticipated in this way actually occurred.

The result: Premonition verified—0 percent

Not verified—100 percent

Conclusion: My so-called premonitions mean nothing.

Of course, if I entertain enough of them, someday one is bound to be on target. But why should I let them disturb my peace?

Battle won.

But the larger struggle continues. From the time a child emerges from the womb until as an old person he takes his last breath, life is a struggle. I want to fight on strong until the end. And then I want that "rich welcome into the eternal kingdom" that Peter anticipated.

TO FINISH WELL, HOW
"PREPARED" MUST ONE BE?

I had *the dream* again just the other night. I recognized it as the recurring dream I have had occasionally over the years, despite the different content, setting and events. In its earlier versions I was just ready to enter the pulpit of my church. A huge crowd had assembled; there was standing room only. I was surprised because this was an ordinary Sunday service. I thought it was great to have so many present. I had prepared my message well. I was ready.

Then a problem arose. To my frustration I couldn't find my Bible or my notes.

In more recent years the same scenario has repeated, except I'm speaking at an overflowing writers conference. The missing necessities are my notes and the handouts to distribute to the conferees. It seems apparent that this is essentially the same dream, just as Pharaoh's dreams, first of stunted cows and then of blasted heads of grain on a stalk, were one (Gen 41:25).

I'm not saying my dreams are prophetic, as Pharaoh's were. I recognize that some version of a dream like mine is common. A woman dreams she is back in school. It's time for class, and her lesson or book is in her locker, which she either can't find or can't open. A man dreams he is to act in a play. The curtain is about to rise, and he doesn't even remotely know his lines.

I long ago decided *the dream* represents something more basic than being caught unprepared for a speech, a class or a drama. It reveals a general fear of being caught short, inadequate to meet life's demands.

My most recent version of *the dream* differed. I was vacationing at a remote spot on the shoreline of a huge body of water, like Washington's Puget Sound. I needed to catch an important flight very soon but had no way or time to reach the airport. The authorities who had scheduled the flight for me knew I was on that shoreline, but it stretches for more than a hundred miles and has all sorts of coves and inlets. There was no way they could find me and no way for me to reach the airport to catch my flight. My situation was impossible.

"Relax," said a companion, unnoticed until now and

still unidentified. "Everything is taken care of. Here, just push the button on this small box. It activates a locator signal. Your helicopter will be here in no time."

I smiled. How simple had been the solution to my "impossible" situation!

I see one significant difference between this latest version and earlier versions of *the dream*. This time the problem is specifically resolved, and all by grace. There is no pressure on me to deliver. Instead of being defeated or triumphing through my own resourcefulness or heroism, I simply press a button. And I have a Companion to direct me even in that.

I must be careful about pressing details of dreams too far. The important trip I must take could be to heaven. Or it could be a journey into old age. It could be something else I can't even guess. That is not something I need to know. What I need to know is that I am prepared for whatever journey lies ahead, not because I do all things well but because I stand before God by grace, accepted in his beloved Son.

I want to make all the preparations I can. But when that is not enough and it's too late to do more, a locator box and a helicopter are all prepared for me, and a Companion to direct my finger to the button.

Meanwhile, I must continue to walk by faith and not by sight, even when dark days come. Such days came to King George VI of Great Britain and his people early in World War II. With Europe fallen to Hitler and with England standing alone against overwhelming odds, King George could not even offer "a light at the end of the tunnel" as he prepared his annual Christmas message to the nation in 1939. Instead, he quoted these lines from "The Gate of the Year" by a little-known American poet, Minnie Louise Haskins:

> I said to the man who stood at the gate of the
>   year,
> "Give me a light that I may tread safely into the
>   unknown."
> And he replied, "Go out into the darkness
> And put your hand into the hand of God.
> That shall be to you better than light,
> And safer than a known way."

That's good enough for me. Personally, I suppose I will

always analyze everything and try to understand it. I am an unrepentant, unreconstructed analytical thinker. But I also know One who already has everything figured out. I am in good hands.

> So I go on not knowing,
> Nor would I if I might.
> I'd rather walk in the dark with God
> Than go alone in the light;
> I'd rather walk by faith with Him
> Than go alone by sight.
> ("He Knows" by Mary G. Brainard)